Visions of My Dreams

Tanya R. Crawford

Copyright © 2012 by Tanya R. Crawford

Visions of My Dreams
by Tanya R. Crawford

Printed in the United States of America

ISBN 9781624197918

All rights reserved solely by the author. The author guarantees all contents are original and do not infringe upon the legal rights of any other person or work. No part of this book may be reproduced in any form without the permission of the author. The views expressed in this book are not necessarily those of the publisher.

Unless otherwise indicated, Bible quotations are taken from King James Study Bible. Copyright © 1988 by Thomas Nelson Publisher.

www.xulonpress.com

12 - October 2013

Jerry R. Crawford

Sis Vernice Carter
Thank you
Praise Be God!

Acknowledgements

Heartfelt thanks to everyone who inspired the writing of this book. Much appreciation to family, friends and supporters who've prayed, read and labored with me.

I thank God for my parents James L. Copes and Dorothy L. Salem. I am especially grateful for Mother Pauline Jordan for her example of love toward the church. The people of the early Greater St. Paul Missionary Baptist Church of Oakland (1956) are to be acknowledged as well.

To my contributors Reverend and Mrs. Willie and Melissa Stewart for paper, typing and copying; my Oakland Public Library friends and The African-American Museum & Library of Oakland, CA, where Shannon McQueen was a great help and resource. Thank you to Ulander (Jan) Russell for everything and Alyce Ford-Gilbert for the years of steadfast support and friendship. The baby is finally here!! Thank you.

To the Saints of all my church affiliations and especially Pastor James E. Anderson Sr. and my church family at Saints' Rest Missionary Baptist Church, you carried me, prodding and praying. Thank you to (Mom) Ollie Douglas, Mother Ruth L. Miner, and especially Sister Bobbie Wakefield for the copying of this manuscript in its early stages. Thank you to Karleen Cathey for sharing the booklet of Xulon Press. Paramount thanks to Samone Nandi, my right hand at the computer and the thriving force toward the completion of this work.

Special thanks to my sisters Liz Harris and Margo Salem for the tireless support of me and my work. Thank you James V. Copes my brother, you were there for much of the early adventures. Love to my brothers Michael Salem and Howard Salem. Love you madly (Nappy) Johnny D. Salem. Thank you to all my nieces, nephews, and the Crawford Family.

To my dear daughter Rachel E. Crawford, you have been with me through the ups and downs of life and the craziness of writing this book. Thanks for your constant help with the manuscript, your patience, advice and prayers.

Lastly for my late husband Archie L. Crawford and son Aaron T. Crawford in heaven, I'll see you again.

To those who were not named, love to you and thank you for your support.

Contents

I. GEMS 11

II. TITLED PIECES 21
- Expectation
- Heaven Is Free
- Light
- Lord, I Am Waiting
- Good Morning
- The Presence of the Lord Is Here
- Heavenly Shoes
- Come, Birds
- Fruits
- Spirit of Mother
- Dreams
- Generations
- God Loves Me
- Music
- A King Cometh
- That Moment
- Lord, Help Me
- When You Go Away
- Give Us This Day
- Vanity
- Friends
- Heavenly Hues
- All Day I Give Thanks
- Power in the Wilderness
- Some New Things
- I Will Wait
- Joy in the Morning

- ➢ Talk to Me
- ➢ Never Alone
- ➢ Praise Is a Must
- ➢ Heavenly Ministers
- ➢ One More Time
- ➢ The Blessing
- ➢ Dancing
- ➢ Complacency
- ➢ Kisses to Heaven
- ➢ My Time
- ➢ Music for God's Ears
- ➢ Heavenly Sounds

III. SING TANGÉ SING 31
- ➢ Rise, Shine, Give God the Glory
- ➢ The Preacher
- ➢ Church Candy

IV. PRAYERS 43
- ➢ A Wisdom Prayer
- ➢ Sunday Morning Devotional Prayer at Home by My Husband, Deacon Archie L. Crawford
- ➢ Sunday Service Prayer by My Husband, Deacon Archie L. Crawford
- ➢ Common Sunday Morning Prayer
- ➢ Fervent Prayer
- ➢ A Prelude of Song and Noon Thanksgiving Prayer
- ➢ A Noonday Prayer for Aaron and Others
- ➢ Tribute Prayer to a Fallen Singer
- ➢ 9/11/2001
- ➢ A Prayer of Deliverance
- ➢ A Healing Prayer
- ➢ Mother's Prayer
- ➢ Pray On, My People

V. INSPIRATIONAL STORIES .53
- ➢ It's in Your Hands
- ➢ Laying On of Hands
- ➢ Stay-the-Sun Moments

Contents

- Come, Holy Spirit
- Who Will Roll the Stone Away?
- Letter to the President (Barack Obama)
- Dare to Dream
- Letter from the President (Barack Obama)

GEMS

GEMS are something of great value; they derive from a half century of journaling. Some pieces are reminiscent of Proverbs. Most depict daily life experiences shared with God.

You are invited to engage, smile and ponder each nugget.

1. Lord, this morning I see time on my face. I see where You have brought me. I see Your hand. I see Your purpose for why You brought me through.
2. Lord, my desire is to put You first in my day, all in between and all through the day, never to forget about You, even when I am asleep.
3. God smiled a little on me today in the amount of forty-two dollars.
4. Jesus, first fix my heart. Then all hearts that touch mine will be at peace.
5. A healing in the city, my God, my God!
6. Lord, this is the beginning; only You know the middle and the end.
7. Lord, please give me the patience and the strength to make it today.
8. There is a bright side somewhere.
9. How strong is your faith?
10. Before the foundation of the world, God put the dreams in my heart.
11. "Come devil, go devil; God send Sunday" (Fletcher Crawford).
12. He gives us only enough for a day. Jesus wants us to come to Him daily. Truly this is the way to renew our relationship with Him.
13. I prayed.
14. "What a friend we have in Jesus" (song).

15. God spoke and He created. So will I.
16. Thank You, Lord. You have provided daily bread—I've been invited out.
17. The number of water pots I put out reflects my faith.
18. Man can write you a check, but if God doesn't endorse it, you can't cash it.
19. Father, if I could empty my soul now with my tears, I would cry.
20. The clouds are the dust of God's feet (Nahum 1:3).
21. Lord, I'm open to Your voice, Your word, and your way.
22. Lord, thank You for the quiet, stolen moments.
23. When I look at each face, I try to remember to see God.
24. Take the opportunity to look into the eyes of the angels that you meet daily; you will see a glimpse of heaven.
25. "Be not forgetful to entertain strangers: for thereby some have entertained angels unaware" (Hebrews 13:2).
26. My father is the king, and I wear a crown.
27. God gives everything, Mother gives most things, and you bring the rest.
28. "This is the day, which the Lord hath made; we will rejoice and be glad in it" (Psalm 118:24).
29. Lord, I know that You are up there, even though the sky is gray.
30. Lord, thank You for this beautiful day.
31. Lord, whatever it takes, whatever they may ask me to do, to pay, I will do it with Your help.
32. Hurry, Lord. Please come.
33. Have you ever looked into the night heaven, acknowledged the moon and the stars and prayed, "Our Father, which art in heaven, hallowed be thy name"? (Matthew 6:9).
34. Lord, let my last days be my best days.
35. Nobody knows the trouble I see.
36. I'm so glad that troubles don't last always.
37. Lord, it is I, standing in the need of prayer.
38. I could not have made it without You.
39. Thank You for quietness, stillness, and Your peace.
40. Lord, I will be careful to give Your name all the praise, glory, and honor.
41. Lord, keep my body strong.

42. God, give me the courage to do what I have to do.
43. I am free. I have finished my course.
44. If you can just hold on!
45. Lord, be with me in my midnight hours.
46. Lord, thank You for sending Your angels to escort me when I was lost.
47. Lord, here I am, weary, wounded, and sad.
48. God There is none like You.
49. Jesus, I don't have to see my way, for You are the way.
50. I'll rest in Your arms today.
51. Fear not, Tanya. Everything is gonna be all right.
52. Lord, thank You for Your friendship.
53. Thank You, Lord, for the sunshine and its warmth, its healing, its brightness.
54. The devil desires to sift me like wheat. Today I feel like I am going through the sieve.
55. I am trusting God for a breakthrough.
56. I am touching and agreeing with heaven.
57. Lord, I thank You for this spirit in this body in this time and place.
58. Lord, smile on everyone who has poured into my life; bless them.
59. Jesus is the answer.
60. Lord, please let this project come to pass. Let it be, Lord. Let it be.
61. I believe!
62. "In times like these" (song).
63. Lord, will any of this generation make it into the kingdom of God?
64. When I'm through going and coming, gone the last mile of the way, hallelujah, glory to God, I'll be at rest!
65. Lord, as the bell rings, please work a miracle for me.
66. My soul, my feet, my whole body dances for joy.
67. "My faith looks up to Thee, Thou Lamb of Calvary" (song).
68. Lord, You inspire and motivate me!
69. Lord, my future is so bright that I need sunglasses.
70. I just say thank You, Lord.
71. You are worthy to be praised!
72. My Father is the king. He is rich. I don't have to want for anything.

Visions of My Dreams

73. Lord, I want You to be in a hurry, to shake the gifts out of me like salt from a shaker.
74. When this earthly body is all used up, I've got a building not made by hands.
75. Lord, I'll do what I can do and that which I cannot do, I'll wait on You.
76. Jesus, I truly know and understand that everything has a reason and a season.
77. When I totally surrendered, prayed, and told God that I didn't know what to do, that is when He gave me an answer—my solution, my direction!
78. Faith produces miracles.
79. Instead of saying, "Why, God?" I am learning to say, "Thy will be done."
80. "It's another Sunday morning been coming long since creation" (Archie Lee Crawford).
81. Nobody but You, Lord, nobody but You.
82. I dare you to ask and believe.
83. Lord, I praise You. Worthy is the Lamb. Jesus, You died and rose for the sin of the world. Worthy is the King of Kings! Hallelujah!
84. Lord, every day Your people are blessed because of Your grace and mercy.
85. "Be still, and know that I am God: I will be exalted among the heathen, I will be exalted in the earth" (Psalm 46:10).
86. "Even from everlasting to everlasting, Thou art God" (Psalm 90:2).
87. "A man's gift maketh room for him, and bringeth him before great men" (Proverbs 18:16).
88. I am just a vessel, an instrument, some clay, but Lord, I will obey. Lord, please work through me by the direction of Your Holy Spirit. Then I will be able to do Thy will with wisdom and power.
89. Go with God.
90. People are more important in life than things.
91. Isn't it amazing how fingertips have eyes?
92. Death is so quiet, so calm, so still.
93. Lord, thank You for the commission of Your angels watching over me day and night in every situation.

Gems

94. Empty moments that no one or nothing can touch—only Jesus through prayer can help me to fill the empty void.
95. How do you hear a voice that gives no audible sound? Yet the heart hears, believes, and acts upon the words of the voice of the Holy Spirit. In time, right on time, the message of the Word unfolds the blessing.
96. Lord, let me use my gifts strong until I go to the grave.
97. Lord, when I ask You, I have nothing to lose, everything to gain.
98. My home has been a place of joy. Some curses did come, but Jesus turned them into blessings.
99. "This is the day, which the Lord hath made; we will rejoice and be glad in it" (Psalm 118:24).
100. Put your trust in the Lord when troubles come—and they will. You will be able to stand.
101. It's okay to borrow. Jesus borrowed a colt and a grave.
102. Man shall not live by bread alone, but by every word that *proceedeth out of the mouth of God*" (Matthew 4:4).
103. A vision: massive purple curtains. "Jesus, Jesus, Jesus"—that is all I could hear.
104. I got in my bed, closed my eyes, and imagined Jesus holding me in His powerful yet tender arms. What peace!
105. A rough summer—I am vulnerable. Next time I will prepare.
106. I am stretching into heaven, reaching. Lord, let Your rays from heaven shine on me. I need Your strength. I need Your power.
107. The church has been my proving ground, my audience, my opportunity; the pastor, my shepherd; the Bible, my way; and the Holy Spirit, my supreme teacher.
108. Sometimes I just open my Bible and read wherever God leads me. I read wherever my eyes land. I read a few verses before and after. Wherever I read, my soul is fed.
109. Lord, every day I am applying You like lotion, like grease, like oil.
110. Father, please help me to be kind, especially in the midst of my own cares and concerns.

Visions of My Dreams

111. God parted the Red Sea; certainly He can make breaks for me.
112. The more you need God, the bigger He is.
113. Let God be God because He does it so well!
114. Lord, help me to look to Your peace, Your joy, in the midst of reality.
115. The sound of water is calming and refreshing.
116. He who teaches must be patient.
117. The scream of a crow gives my Sunday hope.
118. Getting beyond the things that are broken down . . .
119. I ponder my thoughts. My mind wanders far off. My hands wade through the warm soapy water. My task—the dishes.
120. I love your brokenness—bumps, bruises, burns, and scars—I love you.
121. Without steps it is difficult to advance, climb, and ascend unless you have wings.
122. I didn't see anything. I couldn't hear anything. I kept asking. I kept believing. I kept waiting in faith. I waited until hope manifested into substance.
123. The gift to all my friends today is wisdom.
124. Dreams are a dime a dozen; putting them into action is priceless.
125. A few more risings and settings of the sun and my work will be done.
126. I've been calling myself a promoter for so long, I believe that I am.
127. The whole day awaits my chores—the kids, my husband, my job, my church—so seldom time just for me.
128. In life there is pain and glory.
129. Daffodils make me smile.
130. When I am old, I shall wear purple.
131. Just yesterday I was a child.
132. I weep with you at this time; although I am not present, my heart shares your grief. My prayers are with you.
133. We communed with a dying man who was express on his way to heaven.
134. Every spring a mockingbird comes to sing.

Gems

135. Every time a light goes out, I'm reminded to let mine shine a little brighter.
136. Life will kill you!
137. When a rose is given, stop immediately to enjoy it.
138. Celebrate yourself!
139. You have got to act rich before you are.
140. Love is the test of time that binds hearts, souls, and minds.
141. Hear the birds sing, and see the flowers dress for spring.
142. Life is a waiting game.
143. There is a pocket in my heart especially for your love (dedicated to Rachel).
144. When sadness turns into gladness, my soul sings.
145. Through laughter and tears, we add up the years.
146. Oh, the blossoms of spring spring forth as the white hairs of wisdom!
147. Life is so full. Why am I getting the crumbs?
148. There comes a time when a chocolate chip cookie isn't enough.
149. Cotton candy, puffs of meringue, fluffy pillows hang high in the blue heaven.
150. A foundation begins at home.
151. Use what you got!
152. Only the good do I think of people who have poured into my life.
153. When you prepare, the opportunity comes.
154. This is a blessed house.
155. This is the time for letting go.
156. Our trials come to make us strong.
157. Enjoy the fruit in its season.
158. Your own body will betray you.
159. Life is full of peaks and valleys.
160. I am me—proud, strong, and free to be anything I want to be. There are no limitations.
161. When you get old, you can think about the good times and smile.
162. Good morning in heaven, Deacon and Aaron (dedicated to my husband and son).
163. Give honor to whom it is due.

Visions of My Dreams

164. You never get too old to be blessed. Look at Abraham, Sarah, and Colonel Sanders.
165. Inspiration is precious.
166. The older the man, the longer the prayers.
167. Sometimes you have to be selfish to be sane.
168. The days are getting shorter. Now is the time to love.
169. God, thank You for letting my eyes see a beautiful, black-and-gold, fuzzy bumblebee.
170. I shall say what I will have, and I shall have what I say.
171. Because she is, I am.
172. Little vessels can house great treasures.
173. Gray hairs, a carpet of wisdom, silver strands have paved the way of life.
174. Smile and embrace life.
175. Mountains have ears, just speak.
176. If I offend you and you grow, that was good fertilizer.
177. Today I have decided to live the best thankful, faithful, prayerful, fruitful, blessed life ever.
178. You know a tree by the fruit it bears.
179. The stars are heavenly lights.
180. "If I can make January and February, I can March myself" (Ana Crawford).
181. Here, take some of my spirit, my courage, my faith. Use it to be strengthened. Today I am strong. I have enough to share.
182. Now is the time to live your fantasy!
183. Lord, please help me to get my notes off the page and into a book.
184. We want God to bless us today in our own way. He will come another day and bless us in a completely better way.
185. Coffee and incense, my morning pleasures.
186. People give you what they got. If they have love, that's what you get. If they're crazy, that, too, is what they offer.
187. It is quiet all around me. The world is moving right along without me. I am silent, but full of hope.
188. Today I need a solitary place right now. I need Jesus to come cleanse and renew my soul.

189. Lord, why is it that I can instruct others and they gain, but I am unable to help myself?
190. Out of sadness comes joy; out of joy comes the creativity of the soul.
191. Sometimes I don't know what to do in certain situations. I think I will, but I don't. I say I will not, but then I do.
192. Just a few buds, some wild flowers—pick any of those flowers in the garden. Some new life in here certainly would be appreciated.
193. The loveliest birds live in the loveliest places.
194. Do all you can with what you got.
195. Now is the time to heal. Now is the time to love. Love today.
196. When you are in the valley, remember the mountaintop.
197. I give you my harvest full and free; I give you the best. I give you me.
198. You have to talk to yourself, assure yourself that everything is all right.
199. Satan, get behind me. I ain't playing with you today!
200. When there is no breath, no strength, no motion, no sound, we die.
201. I've got books in me. Every night, as I lay down to rest, all the books that I would write conjure up in me.
202. Ah, the sounds of quietness.
203. Children skipping rope with today's hope.
204. Glasses will be broken; words are spoken.
205. Young love, new love, so tender, so sweet.
206. Done burned the bread, done burned the meat. Lord, what is left to eat?
207. Be humble talking to a fool.
208. Love is so big that it never diminishes. Love is so big that it just keeps on giving.
209. A little tree, its branches bent like a willow, its leaves luminous like a thousand copper pennies.
210. When I have action in faith, God shows me the tangible evidence.
211. Lord, thank You for opening doors and especially windows.

TITLED PIECES

Expectation

When something spectacular happens, you have great expectations. You return to the place of blessings, at the same time looking and hoping that the miracle will happen again and again.

Heaven Is Free

Heaven is free. When I don't have a dime, God's blue heaven is free. I can freely lift up my eyes and see the beauty of God's massive blue sky. Oh, the peace and the freedom it gives my soul, not even a care in God's blue heaven. Just God and me as far as my eyes can see. It's all free!

Light

Light, ever shining forth, always glowing.
Light, always leading the way, showing and spotlighting its subjects, always emphasizing.
Light, always directing and identifying, enhancing vision with warmth.
Light, always dispelling darkness.
Light, ever burning true!

Lord, I am Waiting

Lord, I am waiting on You. I am like Elijah by the brook. I am waiting daily for bread. The groceries are almost gone except for a few eggs, a little cheese, and about three slices of lunch meat. Lord, I'm not complaining; I am just explaining. I could make a meal if I had to. Thank You. PS: I'm waiting on You.

Good Morning

Good morning, God,
Good morning, Jesus,
Good morning, Holy Spirit,
Good morning, heavenly host.

The Presence of the Lord Is Here

The visible presence of God's dwelling with His people as the Shekinah glory (Luke 2:9).

Heavenly Shoes

I won't need to look for special shoes anymore; my golden slippers will be just fine in heaven. I'll walk around heaven all day (dedicated to Mother Spears, March 28, 1992).

Come, Birds

Come, birds; sing peace to my tired soul.
Fly on high, then come again.
Singing your songs of joy, make me look up to heaven.
Lift my spirit from the ground.

Fruits

A woman possesses treasures, which a king desires; jewels, which could bring a prince to his knees; fruits, which would make a common man beg.

Spirit of Mother

Thank God for the spirit of a mother. She continues to strive against adversity and shortage. She creates miracles out of small and basic things.

Dreams

Dreams explode at night like popcorn in a popper.
Sometimes my dreams and visions are so exciting that they keep my eyes from sleep.
I dream of all my fantasies and wishes.
I see myself prosperous and full of accomplishments.
When I awake, I am without a dream, without a plan, without motivation, without success.
Lord, please help me to live my dreams during my waking hours.

Generations

While children cry, our dreams die. Oh, but when they laugh, our future is strong.

God Loves Me

When I see the little sparrow pecking here and there, seemingly without a care, I am reminded of God's loving care.
He satisfies every living thing. A sparrow doesn't fall without Him knowing.
God's care of the little sparrow encourages me to remember how much more God cares for me.
I know He is always present to share my every care.

Music

Music is the heartbeat of my soul. Music is the harmony of my peace, my joy, my praise.

A King Cometh

Heavenly Father, I'm looking for my Boaz. Oh no, I take that back. I will receive whomever you send. I know you will send a king!

That Moment

The dark sky highlighted by the stars gives light to the night. Two birds, one black and one white, their wings flutter in flight. Just enough sound and movement to capture that moment in my sight.

Lord, Help Me

I am holding gifts and potential that I have not used. It is like buying clothes, shoes, dishes, furniture, etc., but never taking advantage of them. Lord, help me break free to use my gifts.

When You Go Away

When you go away, know that you have my love. Take it with you. When you go away, my heart is in your departure. When you go away, know that my love will accompany and comfort you across the miles. When you go away, my longing will be satisfied only when you return.

Give Us This Day

Sometimes our blessing are drips and drops. God desires to communicate with us daily all through the day. He wants us to realize that He is the ever-full fountain pouring out blessings, and on Him only must we rely.

Vanity

We gain and lose all through this life. We pick up and put down. We hold on to cherished items, often hoarding, seldom wanting to part with them. If they are not parted from us, assuredly time will make us let them go.

Friends

Good friends. Best friends. Better than wine. Hearts, souls, and minds intertwine, holding life's threads. These are stitches of joy, laughter, loss, and tears of all the years.

Titled Pieces

Heavenly Hues

Thank You, God. You dipped your fingers in burnt orange, goldenrod, and red russet and flung spurts of pink. The heavenly sky, Your backdrop, infused with tones of charcoal and several shades of blue. You painted an Indian summer sunset worthy of ten thousand eyes.

All Day I Give Thanks

Father, it is another day. I thank You for every second, each minute, each hour. I am cognizant to praise You at noon, at 3:00 p.m., 9:00 p.m., and at midnight. I thank and praise You all the day long.

Power in the Wilderness

Preparation begins in the wilderness. In the wilderness, there is fear, emptiness, loneliness, tears, bitterness, hunger, thirst, prostration, crying out, repentance, and pruning. Even in the wilderness, the Holy Spirit is present. He sustains and comforts until the appointed time. When the preparation is fulfilled, when the battle is over, you will come forth with new refreshing, new strength, new joy, unspeakable anointing, and the power to fulfill all things.

Some New Things

Everything around me is old, torn, chipped, cracked, and just plain worn-out. I want better. I really do. I want new things, especially for my children. My husband needs some new clothes, too.

I Will Wait

Waiting on the Lord. How long can you wait? How long should you wait? Wait until He comes with blessings in His right hand.

Joy in the Morning

Black is the color of my tears. Sky-blue is the color of my rejoicing. "Weeping may endure for a night, but joy cometh in the morning" (Psalm 30:5).

Talk to Me

I would say to the compassionate, the learned, the knowledgeable, the wise, the patient, the communicating man, talk to me about such and such. I would sit at his feet to hear and understand great things.

Never Alone

I am not alone.
The Father, the Son, and the Holy Ghost are always with me. Plus, I have an angel encamping about me.

Praise Is a Must

Praise must be given to God, especially in the worst of times, conditions, and places.
Praise must be given to God in a stable, in prison, in standing water, in filth and feces.
Praise must be given to God when there is blood, stench, or even death all around.
Praise must be given to God. Praise is most sincere, most honorable, and most receptive to the heart of God in these dire times.

Heavenly Ministers

Have you ever had a hurting heart? I have. Sometimes I have been quiet and still. Other times I have petitioned heaven in tears.
Have you ever had the presence of glory come and minister to you? Once on my bed of tears, I felt the presence of Jesus Himself pick me up and cradle me in His arms. He wiped all my tears away. He gave me sweet rest.

Another time, I was sitting in meditation and prayer, with closed eyes and an open heart, when the Holy Spirit and angels came, bringing peace and comfort. I could feel their awesome energy and expansion of power all around me. Wholeness overshadowed every ill.

One More Time

I keep missing out on one more time.
I always hope to get back one more time
To say a word
To say a prayer
To do a good deed.
I just cannot seem to have one more time.
I must learn to console myself and be content.
Therefore, I will be mindful
Every time to say and to do
Everything in love.

The Blessing

The blessing of wind be upon you,
Blow three times: ___ ___ ___
The blessing of breath is within you,
Blow seven times: ___ ___ ___ ___ ___ ___ ___

Dancing

Steps
Movement
Sound
Music
Memories
Emotions
Vibrations
Exuberance
Dancing is for love.
Dancing is for thanksgiving.
Dancing is for joy.
Dancing is for blessings.
I dance out of my soul!

Complacency

Throughout the centuries, better people have survived, struggled, suffered, and even died for their phenomenal contributions that are so necessary and so beneficial. Yet the beneficiaries are forgetful, unthankful, and complacent. Let us rise up to meet the challenges of this day. Let us pass the baton, ensuring future generations.

Kisses to Heaven

A couple of great baseball players come to mind for their outward show of appreciation of God. After hitting a home run, they place their fingers to their lips and blow kisses to God. Daily I, too, blow kisses of love, thanks, and appreciation to my heavenly Father.

My Time

Now is my time
My time for life
My time for love
My time for thanksgiving
My time for praise
My time for health
My time for joy
My time for laughter
My time for rest
My time for dreams
My time for giving
My time for fulfillment.

Music for God's Ears

God loves singing and the playing of instruments. He ordained these gifts in heaven. They exalt His glory in heaven and on earth. He stops to listen to our sincere notes of praise. Whether we sing acappella, accompanied by instrument, in concert or solo, God adores our serenade.

Heavenly Sounds

In heaven the sounds are too wonderful for the ears of men. But the heavenly host makes oblation—"Holy, holy, holy"—continually before God.

Easter Sunday Morning 1956

I have shared on these pages our traditions ordinances, prayers, praise, and worship; preserved from the prospective and testimony of a young black girl.

Sing Tangé sing

The year was 1955. *"Sing, Tangé, sing"*. These were the words ringing in my six-year-old ears. These words have the ability to transport me back to my parents, upbringing, life experiences, my deep roots in Christianity, the church, and its people. My brother James and several other children rehearsed in the Harbor Homes projects. This preparation was for the children's choir of Greater Saint Paul Missionary Baptist Church of Oakland, California. The proud people of the church, most of whom had come from the Southern states, were well acquainted with hard work, especially the cotton fields. These were the people of faith and hope who sought a better life in California. These members were willing to make great physical and financial sacrifices to own a beautiful sanctuary for worship.

The majority of the church members were a part of "The Second Great Migration"[1a] from 1941 through 1970. This was a time when "more than five million African Americans moved to cities in the North, Midwest and West. . . . Many came to work right here in the Bay Area, specifically Oakland, California."[1b] More importantly, the United States of America entered World War II in 1941. The war prompted a great outcry for enlistment. Men of Greater St. Paul answered the call, my husband being one of them. During the war, "the U.S. Maritime Commission had a dire need to find workers to produce a large number of Victory Ships and Liberty Ships."[2a] Mass production was needed around the clock. Despite the need, "minorities and women were not hired."[2b]

In 1941, "black clergymen threatened to organize 50,000 African American laborers to march on Washington DC."[2c] The same year, President Roosevelt thought it incumbent to respond with "executive order 8802."[2d] This law banned "racial discrimination in the field of defense work opportunities."[2e] Now the floodgates were open. "Between 1942 and 1945 nearly 500,000 African Americans migrated to California."[2f] "This was the largest voluntary westward migration of African Americans from the South to California in the nation's history."[2g] Right here in California, the great battleships were made at "Moore Dry Dock of Oakland and Kaiser Shipyards of Richmond."[2h] Many Blacks were employed in these yards during and after World War II. My husband, along with a great number of men from our congregation, worked and retired from Moore's shipyard.

I account and record this history because it is paramount to me and to those who were a part of this era. It is also important to illuminate the caliber and the spirit of the people whom I lived, loved, and worshipped with. My mother taught me to pray before I was five years of age. My brother and I would kneel and recite, "Now I lay me down to sleep. / I pray the Lord my soul to keep. / If I should die before I wake, / I pray the Lord my soul to take." I always added, "God bless Mommy, Daddy, Brother, my friends, and the whole world. Amen." As a child, I would look up into the night sky, looking at the moon and the stars while talking to God. I knew that He loved me. I felt so special. I could talk to Him about any and everything. I remember hearing people say that He never sleeps.

> Yes, Jesus loves me.
> Yes, Jesus loves me.
> Yes, Jesus loves me,
> For the Bible tells me so.

That little song resounded in my head. Many times when I was sad, that song gave me comfort. I believed it; I knew Jesus loved me no matter what.

In 1953, my parents divorced; I did not understand. I did know that I missed my father's presence. I had feelings of hurt. My father moved to San Francisco; that didn't stop our father from being a part of our lives. He came to visit and was faithful at school events. My brother and I often talked with Dad by phone. My most endearing times were when we spent the night in his San Francisco apartment. If I think hard enough and breathe in deeply, I can still smell his cigarettes and strong coffee.

At night we would pile into bed with our father. He would get up in the middle of the night to polish and buff our shoes. I saw him chewing his tongue as he worked. I remember him rubbing his nose against ours and saying, "This is the way the Eskimos kiss." We would laugh at this. Sometimes our father would take us on wonderful outings in San Francisco: the zoo, the beach, Golden Gate Park, ice skating, and Macy's, where we had many shopping sprees. I never wanted our time to end.

He grew up in Minden, Louisiana, in a home where there was no indoor plumbing, no electricity. He read by an oil lamp. Dad told me he was ashamed of that way of living. His father, Vanderbilt Copes, was a dark, tall, and thin man who worked as a porter on the Southern Pacific Railroad. His wife, Evelyn, was a homemaker, a quiet and meek soul. She had a love for horticulture. Grandmother was praised for her lovely hydrangea, lavender in color.

When my father and his brother John returned from World War II, they paid off the home and remodeled it with plumbing and electricity. These additions to the home left both parents comfortable, taking care of their needs and desires.

Soon after the war, my dad went to California. He graduated from the University of California, Berkeley in June of 1949, the same year I was born. Dad had a propensity for law. He attended Hasting School of Law in San Francisco. Although Dad didn't complete law school he believed that education and knowledge triumphed ever level of ignorance, poverty, and discrimination.

Later, when I became an adult, I sensed and recognized his feelings of disappointment for not pursuing his dream to become a lawyer. He never really talked about it. My father worked for the U.S. Postal Service until he retired on February 29, 1976.

After his death in 1998, among his belongings I found a black-and-white photograph of him, along with other distinguished-looking gentlemen, sitting with the Honorable Thurgood Marshall, the first African American Supreme Court justice.

My mother talked often of my father. She always spoke well of him: "He was never late with child support." Dad gave above and beyond his duty. During the holiday seasons, Mother would assist my brother and me in writing our names on the cards to Dad.

Mother, Dorothy Lee, was born May 6, 1926, in Tulsa Oklahoma to the parents of Jody and Ella Quillings, the first of this union. Brother Raymond and sister Elzater followed. Mom grew up with the responsibility of caring for her siblings. She also cooked, cleaned, and assisted her mother with canning fruits and vegetables and making jelly. My grandmother took jars of her bounty to the sick.

As a young girl in elementary school, Mom escaped her mundane life by reading anything around her. Drawings and sketching she loved. Oftentimes she would get into trouble for using all her school paper.

In her pre-teens, Mother left Tulsa. She took a memorable train ride to visit her father on the South Side of Chicago. Her father, divorced from her mother, now returned to the first woman he married and their sons. Mother realized that she was only there for a visit; her place was not there. She returned to Tulsa, where she graduated from Booker T. Washington High School in Oklahoma in 1944.

She dreamed of traveling and being free to experience life on her own terms. Mother was not allowed to dance or go to parties. She did attend a few church socials at Greater Union Baptist Church in Tulsa.

Shortly after graduation, Mother went to California. She had no family there, but Mother made friends easily. She was eighteen, very charming and statuesque. A woman who appreciated fashion, when she wore a hat, you noticed! Mom owned many pairs of high-heeled shoes from Rocsil's. One of her first accounts was with this fine shoe store in downtown Oakland. In 2009, Rocsil's celebrated one hundred years of excellent service to its customers.

Bright lights and late nights intrigued my mom. Dancing

became a newfound love; she kicked up her heels at the renowned Sweet's Ballroom in Oakland, California. This place was a renaissance for big band, swing, and jazz. The marquee highlighted such greats as Lionel Hampton, Benny Goodman, Tommy Dorsey, Billie Holiday, and Duke Ellington. Aside from Mother's social life, she knew the value of making a life for herself and later her children.

Nursing was her chosen profession, eventually becoming a registered nurse (RN). Kaiser Hospital Oakland was one of her work sites. Senior-care facilities were other places of her service. Private care was truly her niche. Mother served with compassion and exemplary care. Her patients and their families loved and rewarded her greatly.

While my mother prepared for her career, my brother and I were entrusted to Pauline Jordan for our primary care for two years. Mother Jordan was a caregiver for children. While the other children would go home at night, my brother and I remained at Mother Jordan's. Mother Jordan was a God-loving and God-fearing soul. A widowed grandmother in her fifties, she already had three grown children and was raising a granddaughter, Bunnie.

Mother Jordan's devotion to Jesus kept our lives involved with church activities from Sunday to Sunday. Mother Jordan became a founding member in the organization of the Greater St. Paul Missionary Baptist Church. "While at Greater St. Paul she held positions in the following groups; St. Paul Circle, C.M. Anderson Circle, General Mission, Baptist Training Union, Sunday School, Teacher's Meeting, Wednesday Prayer Group, and the Mother's Board. She was also active with The Progressive District Association where she was President of the Missionary Society and The Mother's and Deaconess' Board. Mother Jordan was a willing worker, supportively participating in church programs. She never refused a task because she was already too busy, or because she was too tired. Her 35 year Membership at Greater St. Paul is recognition of her dedication."[3]

I am most grateful and thankful for the presence of Mother Jordan in my life. She took me to the House Of The Lord. It was she who watered my faith in Jesus with a song. My Mother always pronounced my name "Tan-Ya." I do not know why but Mother Jordan changed my name she began to call me "Tangé." Her encouragement, "Sing Tangé sing", prompted me to lift my voice in melodious notes, using words to acknowledge, to praise, and to thank God for all His blessings.

While going to the house of the Lord on Sunday was the primary worship day, there were other noteworthy meetings and activities held at the church as well as in the homes of the members.

There were weekly and monthly meetings. The pastor met with the deacons and teachers weekly. The various choirs rehearsed on their specific evenings. Business meetings were held monthly, and children were not present. The general mission also met once a month. Away from the church, the mission circles gathered, sometimes a couple of times a month. The circles were named after women in the Bible, like Deborah, Ruth, and Naomi. I was present at a few of these meetings. I recall mainly middle-aged women and up. A Bible lesson would be discussed; reports on the sick and charity accounts would be given. After all the business was concluded, refreshments were served. Occasionally little sandwiches, yummy pound cake, or homemade cookies were prepared. Coffee and tea would be offered in lovely china.

One of my most fun experiences was at a, "Heaven and Hell" party held at a member's home. A bag was used to hold slips of paper marked either heaven or hell. One would pay a dollar per pull. A heavenly pull entitled one to ice cream and cake. They would recite a scripture. Chili and crackers were served to the hell bound. They would debate the scriptures. There was lots of talking and laughter among the men and women. Few children were present, only those who didn't have a sitter. We were in another room. But I heard and saw most of the action. I also ate my share from "heaven" and "hell." The funds went back to the church.

My thoughts return to Sunday, a day to reverence The Lord all day. On Sunday we arose early to get scrubbed up, ate breakfast, and dressed in our Sunday best. Mother Jordan reminded my brother and me of proper conduct and the sacredness of our pilgrimage to The Lord's House. We all looked forward to the fellowship with the saints, family, and community. Together we thanked God for His goodness and praised and worshipped Him. This day was full of tradition—the same order of service Sunday after Sunday, year after year. In the morning, Sunday school was the first service. Classes convened all over the sanctuary and in classrooms. There were classes for the youngest child to the oldest adult.

In Sunday school, my favorite lessons were the ones of miraculous actions, such as Moses parting the Red Sea, Noah's ark and the animals, David and Goliath, and Jesus' healing of all the sick people. Sunday school was a time to be with all my friends. Everyone wore his or her Sunday best. The cotton dresses were starched and ironed, with beautiful white collars and tied sashes. I felt very special when I wore my nylon lace dress. The girls had pressed hair with big bows and greased legs with lace socks. Sometimes the shoes were patent leather. Other times the girls wore bucks and other leather shoes as opposed to the canvas tennis shoes worn throughout the week. The boys had short haircuts and shiny faces. They wore suits with white and colored starched shirts and bow ties. Young boys sported slacks and leather shoes. Most of us were either missing teeth or were snaggletooth, but we were smiling just the same.

After Sunday school, there would be a break. There was a store near the church. The older kids would go and smuggle back treats at our request. We secretly chewed, shared and traded gum and candy away from the adults, out of fear that our treats would be taken away. During service we kids would try to sit together. We whispered and passed notes until we were caught. Once the service started, there was no walking and talking. We had to go to the restroom before service began. If the adults had to go out after, they would tiptoe out with their back slightly bent, holding up the right hand with only the pointer finger in the air as a way of asking to be excused. Sometimes an older woman or someone's Mom would give us that look, like "I'll Kill You!" And do not let them come over to you with their mouth not moving, talking under their breath; you knew that you had better hush. They did not play. Sometime they just separated us.

At 11:00 a.m., the real excitement began. The choir would come in robed and rocking, especially the members of the younger choirs. There were numerous choirs for designated Sundays. There was the Senior Choir, Choir 2, The Mission Chorus, The Inspirational Choir (my favorite), and the Youth and Children's Choir, which my brother and I were a part of. I must also mention the Saint Paul Specials, a group of men who sang many of the late Reverend James Cleveland's songs. John Perkins, one of the members of the group, could sing "Stood on the Banks of Jordan" with a voice as smooth as Luther Vandross. The piano and organ accompanying this great singing made praise glorious.

On the first Sunday of the month, the day was long. We were at church from sunup to sundown. We worshiped, ate, played, and napped until evening service culminated with baptism and communion.

After the morning service, we had a sumptuous spread. Mother Jordan and some of the members who remained at the church brought food with them on Sunday morning, which was prepared and packed the night before. There was usually fried chicken, potato salad, a container of greens, yams, cornbread, "light bread," which was white, jelly cakes, chocolate and pound cakes. Occasionally we had sweet-potato pie or lemon-meringue pie. You talk about good eating. What a feast and fellowship! We all ate food and drank Kool-Aid until we were bloated and about to pop.

After eating, we kids played outside on the church grounds. Simon Says and Mother, May I? were the most fun games. When we were all played out, we would nap in the church on the pallets in the classrooms. Soon it was time for the Baptist Training Union, or the BTU. At this meeting, the elders would talk to the youth about church protocol, how to speak, and how we should conduct ourselves. Often there was a Bible drill. The drill's objective was for the young people to be familiar with the books of the Bible in order to find the given scripture and read it as quickly as possible. Evening service was the epitome of true church worship. During these services, we faithfully and dutifully commemorated the two principal ordinances of the Baptist Church: Baptism and Communion (The Lord's Supper).

The women, mainly older mothers and deacon's wives, would be in white dresses, their heads covered in white caps, hankies, or hats. These women were alert and prepared to respond to any beck and call. These elder women were responsible for the elements and the set-up of the communion table. They also dressed and assisted the candidates for Baptism. An aspirant would oftentimes wear a white robe or gown. Other times women and men would be baptized in whatever they brought. White sheets and towels were held by the attending women. It appeared that most of those baptized were children. However, I do recall seeing older adults, "grown folks," being immersed in the pool. With my eyes as a child, I can still see the honorable elders. The men appeared as tall as trees. They were dressed in black suits and crisp white shirts, black neckties and polished black shoes.

The pastor, Reverend J. P. Reed, along with a deacon, usually Brother Archie L. Crawford, would assist in the baptismal pool. The same deacon, who possibly baptized me as a child, later became my husband. When baptizing, the pastor could call down Heaven to Earth. He had a way of looking beyond you and saying, "I wish you could see." That preacher would lift one hand to the throne of God and His Son Jesus, and with the other hand on the candidate, he'd say, "Obedience to the great Head of the church. I baptize you, my brother [or sister], in the name of the Father, the Son, and the name of the Holy Ghost." It was like the day of Pentecost—men and women shouting, running, hats and purses flying, ushers advancing with fans and kleenex. Oh, what a hallelujah time! When the people could regroup, songs such as "At the Cross," "The Old Rugged Cross," and "There Is a Fountain" were sung. This was a very solemn and sacred time.

The communion table ("This do in remembrance of Me") would be prepared prior to the service. The preacher and the deacons would wash their hands in the same basin. They dried their hands with the same white towel. The white cloth of secrecy shrouded the communion table. It was as if Jesus' body was literally there. The men would officiate behind the held-up cloth. Silver trays were held forth bearing broken pieces of flat, unleavened bread. Slotted silver trays bore the thimble-sized individual cups filled with grape juice.

Before The Lord's Supper, a deacon would offer a fervent prayer. A scripture was read pertaining to The Supper. The communion was served in courses: first the newly baptized, then the choir, the congregation, the mothers, the deacons, and then the pastor would be last to receive the sacrament.

As we held our bread and juice, the pastor would recite, "This is My body, which is broken for you. This do in remembrance of Me." We all ate the bread. Likewise, he took the cup, saying, "This is My blood, which is shed for the remission of sin. This do in remembrance of Me." All the baptized believers drank together.

We sang a hymn and departed.

> I know it was the blood
> I know it was the blood
> I know it was the blood for me.
> One day when I was lost
> He died upon the cross
> I know it was the blood for me.

Still today on Sundays, especially first Sundays, link me right back to my beginning—my family, the saints, my faith, my joy, my strength, and my song.

Rise, Shine, Give God the Glory

In the shadow of my mind, I can still see that old woman, her ebony skin weathered and taut. More clearly, I hear her morning revelry. She faithfully marched through the housing project, lifting her strong alto voice, singing:

> Rise, shine, give God the glory, glory.
> Rise, shine, give God the glory, glory.
> Rise, shine, give God the glory,
> Soldiers of the cross.

I am sure that she alarmed some, but blessed so many more. For me, this mysterious woman brought joy. I was glad to hear her voice in song.

Mothers were encouraged; they lovingly and intentionally aroused their children from their sleep. These women nurtured and equipped their children to go forth like good soldiers.

Children were eager to arise to embrace the blessings as well as the battles unfolding on the carpet of destiny.

> Rise, shine, give God the glory, glory.
> Rise, shine, give God the glory, glory.
> Rise, shine, give God the glory,
> Soldiers of the cross.

The Preacher

> The reverend one
> The sincere man of God
> The bearer of the Word
> The bearer of the Bible
> The bearer of the Good News.
> The black suit
> The stiff, starched, well-ironed white shirt
> The black tie
> The black hat
> The black spit-shined shoes.
> The simplicity
> The wisdom
> The anointing
> The power!
> The old preacher,
> The preacher of old.

Church Candy

The bearers of the peppermints, the righteous church candy. Observe any elder mothers of the church aged sixty and above, especially those seventy through ninety, and they have peppermints.

Oh yeah, the younger women, the "sisters," have mints, usually Tic Tacs, Certs, Altoids, some new products, and occasionally a peppermint.

But if you're talking authentic church candy, see a mother. The peppermint might be round, wrapped, unwrapped, a colossal pillar smashed into smithereens, or Christmas candy canes broken or bitten. It might even be old, faded, with lint, or even sticky, but it's a peppermint.

For years I have noticed that these peppermints are liberally passed out to some. The pastor, preachers, deacons, and a few choir members—they are automatically given this candy.

I don't know if the mothers are concerned about fresh breath or giving aid to those who preach, pray, and sing. It could even be a token of love.

Sometimes the matronly women pacify or treat a child with a peppermint. I'm not sure when and where this tradition started, but it is still going strong.

Ask any elder mother of the church for a mint and she will gladly pull out a tattered plastic bag or an old handkerchief and say, "Here, baby. Here's a peppermint."

PRAYERS

A Wisdom Prayer

Alone, newly divorced, afraid of life, I knew that I needed God's guidance.

The Bible was such a great comfort to me. The Word contains gems of knowledge and pearls of wisdom. This book was my hope and a road map for life.

I returned to my original church membership. There I was baptized as a child. It seemed easier to get closer to God being with familiar people.

The recommitment to the Word of God through Christ Jesus and the church fellowship inspired me to read my Bible and pray more. Life had questions. And I needed answers. I read that Solomon was the wisest man. I, too, wanted wisdom.

One very special night, I saw King Solomon. He was a wide, dark man sitting on a golden throne. Black disclike objects covered his eyes. He wore a fabric cap, like a yarmulke. Solomon's attire was rich of color and texture. His garment was gold, red, and purple with metallic threads woven through the fabric. King Solomon never said a word. He just nodded his head.

When I awoke, I knew that God had answered my prayer. He had given me the gift of wisdom.

Sunday Morning Devotional Prayer at Home by My Husband,
Deacon Archie L. Crawford

Preface

This prayer or a similar prayer was prayed each Sunday morning around the dining room table, with my husband leading the prayer and the children and I present. We would bow in prayer before eating and leaving for morning worship at the church.

Prayer

"Lord, I thank You for waking me up early this morning and letting my eyes see a brand-new day. Father, it is another Sunday morning that has been coming long since creation. I thank You for my wife and children. Lord, bless my family. Thank You for food, shelter, and raiment. Thank You for every good and perfect gift, which comes from above. Lord, bless us this day to get out to Your house. Strengthen and bless us to do Thy will. Take care of us as we go. In the name of Jesus I pray. Amen".

Sunday Service Prayer by My Husband,
Deacon Archie L. Crawford

Heavenly Father, once more and again I come before You like an empty pitcher before a full fountain.

Lord, I thank You that You enabled me to look out and see a brand-new day. Thank You from my earliest existence up until this present moment. Hundreds by thousands have quit the walk of life, but You let my golden moments roll on a little while longer. Thank You.

If I had ten thousand tongues, I couldn't thank You enough. The cattle on a thousand hills belong to You. All the fish at sea, the world and they that dwell therein, all the silver and gold, houses and lands, they belong to You. Please, Sir, have mercy.

Lord Jesus, please bless everyone under the sound of my weak voice. Bless the pastor, the preached Word, the pulpit, the deacons, mothers, officers, members, the whole congregation. Bless the musicians to play well on the instruments. Bless the choir to sing Zion songs.

Bless the sick and afflicted all over the land and country. Lift up bowed-down heads, and mend broken hearts. I know that You can do it. I know You are a heart fixer and a mind regulator. You are slow to anger and plenteous in mercy. Please, Sir, have mercy.

I know that You are God and beside You there is no other. Lord, I know that You've got all power. You came down through forty-two generations, Lord. You speak and men die; You speak and they live again.

Jesus, one day pity brought You down to this sinful world. You went to the cross for the sin of the world. On the cross You hung, bled, and died. It got dark, and the whole earth rocked and reeled like a drunken man.

They put Your body in a borrowed tomb. It stayed there three days and three nights. But early Sunday morning, You got up with all power. Thank ya! And now, Lord, when it's all over down here, come so close that I can lay my head upon Your breast and breathe out my life sweetly there. Then give me a home in Thy kingdom where I can serve You throughout eternity, where every day will be Sunday and Sabbath will have no end. No more trouble, heartaches, and pain. No more death and tears. Jesus will wipe away all tears. It will be all over. Just howdy, howdy and never good-bye. Thank ya! [with shouting and tears]

Common Sunday Morning Prayer

Father in heaven, I come with my knees bent and body bound, trying to turn You some 'umble thanks.

You woke me up early this morning, and I was clothed and in my right mind. When I rose, I said, "Thank You, Lord. I thank You that my bed wasn't my cooling board, my sheets weren't my winding sheets, the four walls weren't my grave. Thank You for a reasonable portion of health and strength."

Father, forgive me of all unrighteousness. If You find anything like sin around my heart, please remove it and love my soul freely again.

Lord, bless this church, the pastor, and all the people.

Bless those that don't know You in the pardon of their sins.

Now, Lord, let Your Word be preached so that some man, woman, boy, or girl might come running, saying, "What must I do to be saved?"

And now, Lord, I might be in my home or on the streets of town, I might be on the highway, I might be in my sick room, but Lord, wherever I am, please cross me over Jordan in a calm time.

Saints, I'm going to my heavenly home that the Lord has prepared for me. I'm going where the wicked shall cease from troubling and the weary shall be at rest. I'll see the man who died and rose for me. I'll see Jesus face-to-face. Glory hallelujah! Amen.

Fervent Prayer

Our Father, which art in heaven, hallowed be Thy name. Thy kingdom come, Thy will be done, on earth as it is in heaven. Give us this day our daily bread, and forgive us our debts, as we forgive our debtors. And lead us not into temptation, but deliver us from evil, for thine is Yo kingdom, the power, and *the* glory forever.

Lord, I know that you are prayer-hearing God 'cause you heard and answered my prayers.

Lord, bless this church. Bless the pastor and every home that's represented here. Lord, bless my home and my grandcheer-in. Take care of them. Lord, give me strength. Lord, ease "racking" pain. Bless every church dough open in Yo name.

Lord, I'm leaning and depending on You. We can't do nothing without Yo Holy Spirit. We can't pray, we can't sing, without You.

Jesus, we need You this morning. Let Yo Holy Spirit take over. Let Yo will be done. Help us to be in one accord. Please, Father, have mercy. Lord, thank You for saving my soul. Mercy reached yo throne, and pity bought You down low. You died on the cross. Then You rose with all power.

Lord, when it's all over down here, when I can't do no more, Lord, meet me in my dying room. Lord, don't leave me. Just give me a home in Yo kingdom, just anywhere, anywhere, so I can praise You throughout eternity.

In Jesus' name I pray [shouting], "Thank You, thank You!"

A Prelude of Song and Noon Thanksgiving Prayer

Dr. Mike Murdock inspired me to sing a love song to the Lord before prayer.

Now at noon I sing to Jesus. This is one of my favorite songs to Him.

Prelude: "I Love You" by Edwin Hawkins

> I love You, I love You,
> I love You, Lord, today;
> Because You cared for me in such a special way.
> And yes, I praise You,
> I lift you up,
> I magnify your name;
> That's why my heart is filled with praise.

Lord, I have come to know You in all times; in all situations, I thank You. I look forward to our time together. I let no one or nothing stop me at our appointed time.

I long to come to You, to praise You, to exalt Your holy and righteous name. I bless heaven. I tell You how wonderful, how awesome, how great You are! Lord, You take my breath away; You fill me with such love, joy, thanksgiving, such peace and hope. My cup runs over.

I cannot contain myself. I just thank You. I will praise You all the days of my life—forever. Lord, I lift my hands in total praise. I love You, Lord. Amen.

A Noonday Prayer for Aaron and Others

In 1996, by the inspiration of the Holy Spirit, prayer at noon was instituted in my school office. The Holy Spirit specifically told me to pray for my son Aaron. I turned my face to the wall; I called it my "wailing wall." There I prayed for Aaron, the community, and others.

Prayer was much needed during this difficult time in my son's life. My Aaron was a beautiful, loving son, full of joy, energy, and love for all. He was nurtured in a loving Christian family environment. Aaron accepted Jesus at an early age and was baptized. He was a young preacher.

Life became difficult for Aaron after the death of my husband, his father. My son loved being outside with his friends. Aaron chose a life that was different from his upbringing. Still, he knew that his sister Rachel and I and the rest of the family loved him. Aaron knew that at noon I was praying for him.

"Prayer is the key; faith unlocks the door." My office was a prayer station for others and for myself as well. I talked to Jesus about the children, their parents, the teachers, and the community at large. Coworkers and parents knew that I prayed at 12:00 p.m. They dared not interrupt. On numerous occasions, staff and parents would come before noon and we would petition the Lord. Sometimes there were tears and rejoicing for the victory of our spoken and answered prayers. I continued my noon prayer for Aaron until he was murdered on May 23, 2003.

I told Jesus that I could not talk to Him anymore in the same way. I learned to petition Him in a new way, a new spirit. I thank God for Aaron's new life. I'm not at the school anymore, yet the school remains in my heart. However, wherever I am, if I am cognitive of the noon hour, I pause to acknowledge my Father. I continue my prayer for family, others, and myself.

Tribute Prayer to a Fallen Singer

Lord, may I never feel hopeless enough to take my own life. At times I have wanted to give up and let go, but I just could not. I even wished for wings to fly away to be at rest.

There were times that my faith was so small; I was afraid that if I dropped my mustard seed, I would not be able to find it again.

Thank God that I can walk by faith and not by sight. Lord, please help my unbelief.

In every situation, all circumstances, every problem, I must know that You, Lord, are a very present help in the time of trouble.

Father, when I am not able to ask You for help, please remember me. You promised! Without You, I, too, would be without hope.

Committing suicide must be a subconscious act, void of discerning Your presence, Your love, and Your omnipotence.

Prayers

9/11/2001

My God, My God,
Help us. Save us.
This great land and its people have been violated.
The whole earth is trembling. America is crumbling and on fire.
Smoke and darkness cover us.
Suicide bombers demolished the Twin Towers.
We are in shock and disbelief.
People are perishing.
We languish.
Our tears are very great.
Lord, please have mercy.
Those on the scene of that horrific day,
Along with police and firefighters who came to aid,
Many lost their lives.
God, where is our safety?
Where is our help?
The same day, the passengers of Flight 93 were commandeered by evil men.
Courageous men and women sacrificed their lives for others.
God, You know all about it.
Lord, You said You would avenge the perpetrators.
Help us, Lord, to forgive those who trespass against us.
Father, rest the souls of those who instantly came into Your holy and glorious presence.
Please bless the families, loved ones, friends, and coworkers of those slain.
Lord, please help America; we are in trouble.
Dear Lord, bless and keep us.
Amen!

A Prayer of Deliverance

Lord Jesus,
Someone is calling on You because they are so sick.
Someone is calling on You because they are in trouble.
Someone is calling on You because they are afraid.
Someone is calling on You because they need finances.

Someone is calling on You because they are being abused.
Someone is calling on You because they are in prison.
Someone is calling on You because they are bereaved.
Father,
Someone is calling on You because they are lost.
Jesus, please have mercy.
Amen!

A Healing Prayer

Lord, it is I.
I need You.
I am broken.
I am wounded.
I am weak.
My heart and eyes are full of tears.
I tried to console and conceal my tears, but I could not.
Lord, I need healing.
I want to be whole.
I need a refreshing.
I need restoration.
Lord, I know that You are able.
Master, would You please bless and heal me right now?

Mother's Prayer

When I go to sleep and you cannot wake me, you must know that I am with the loving and comforting Jesus. Heaven is a beautiful place.

I know that you will be sad; you will cry and miss me sorely. It is okay to weep for a while. In time your tears will turn into precious memories of joy.

Children, my beloved children, just remember and know that I will always be with you every day of this life, even in death, all the way to eternity. Our love will never die because Jesus is alive and He holds life and death.

Remember all the good things that you were taught. Never forget God's Word. His Word is your road map, your peace, joy, wisdom, and success for living now. By accepting Jesus as your Savior, He is your ticket to eternity.

Until then, just believe and know that I will always love you. In heaven I will know all things. I will see you in heaven.

Love,
Mother

Pray On, My People

Far away, long ago on the continent of Africa, prayers came from a people of gratitude, knowledge, wealth, and freedom.

Conversations addressed to the God of heaven and earth, the Creator who created everything and everybody.

Pray on, My people.

Then the earth trembled and shook: the oceans vomited up the blood of my people. My God, my God!

Supplications rendered from a people of anguish, deportation, incarceration, slavery, oppression, and struggle.

Prayers prayed in silence, uttered in cries, moaning, groaning; and requests sown in tears of sorrow, sometimes tears of joy for the hope of deliverance.

These prayers from a diaspora of hopeful people continued in the new land. In every situation, in every place, the people talked with God.

Pray on, My people.

God knew us, loved us, heard our cries, and blessed us at all times. Yes, deliverance and freedom came again to God's people.

Education, skills, jobs, human and civil rights, opportunity, and higher knowledge were afforded to these new Americans.

We became inventors, owners, entrepreneurs, and philanthropists. All these achievements have been accomplished by the grace of God through Jesus Christ.

Pray on, My people.

The prayers of My people have been full of faith, hope, and love to a loving and compassionate God who gave His only begotten Son, Jesus, who loved us so much that he shed His blood on Calvary for the remission of sin; the third day He rose with all power.

Pray on, My people.

Now there is salvation, justification, sanctification, and glorification to come for those who have accepted Jesus as Savior.

Jesus now sits at the right hand of God, making intercession for us. We now know that the Holy Spirit helps us to pray in the will of God through Jesus.

Pray on, My people.

Throughout the generations from the motherland to this land, in fields, secret places, homes, churches, and public places, our people have beseeched the heavenly Father.

Black prayers full of emotion and movement, often preceded by the singing of a hymn or short meter (pause-sing, "I . . . know the Lord will answer prayer"), at times a moan. The droning sound of a hum stirring our souls and encouraging our hearts so that we overflowed with rejoicing and shouting!

Many of the prayers are common and familiar over the land and country. You hear these same prayers being prayed in church after church by the elders. That old deacon, the mother—their words, phrases, and actions culminating like smoke rising to make sweet offering before our Father's throne.

And now, Lord . . .

Whatever our request, we as a people know how to call upon the name of the Lord, the one who sits high and looks low, the God who hears and answers our prayers.

Pray on, My people . . .

INSPIRATIONAL STORIES

It's in Your Hands

Have you ever wondered why the same foods, the same ingredients, can taste so different? I have found the secret.

Bacon and eggs are a very common, simple breakfast. At home or out, I enjoy the paired delights. When I prepare bacon and eggs, the taste differs from my daughter's cooking.

How about trying to make someone else's recipe? Did yours turn out just like theirs? Well, I tried making my husband's hot-water cornbread with him standing at my side. I followed every instruction as he watched. My bread was good, but not the same as his.

Pound cake is another favorite to prepare. By the way, I pray over my cooking, especially when I'm making a cake; each stroke is a prayer and a blessing to all those who will partake. I've noticed that everyone's pound cake, even the texture, is unique.

Yeah, I hear you thinking. My mom used to say, "I heard you before your foot hit the bridge." In other words, you're saying if all factors are measurable and controlled, etc., etc., then why shouldn't everyone's cooking taste the same?

The proof is in the "gnawing of the bag," or the pudding. Truly the revelation concerning this matter came to me days after a profound discussion with a dear friend. As I sat and reflected, I heard the Holy Spirit saying, " The seasoning is in the hands." Yes, I believe that! Your DNA flavors your cooking. God gives each person a gift, which cannot be duplicated.

"And let the beauty of the Lord our God be upon us: and establish thou the work of our hands upon us; yea, the work of our hands establish thou it" (Psalm 90:17).

Laying On of Hands

I believed; I had a need. I made a request, and I received the blessings wrought through my hands by the power of the Holy Spirit.

One day I got the notion that I could use my hands for a blessing and healing. Time and circumstance tested my faith.

When I was a young woman in my twenties and couldn't afford to pay for repairs, I would lay my hands on my car, washer, and refrigerator, asking in the name of Jesus to make those inoperative machines work again. My prayers were affirmed.

In 1995, my dog was sick; he would not eat or stand. The poor dog lay in a corner. After two days of this behavior, my husband bundled the dog in a blanket and carried him to the car. The children and I accompanied him to the pet emergency hospital

The veterinarian briefly examined our dog. He stated that the dog should be kept overnight for observation, and the cost would be approximately a thousand dollars. I thanked the doctor and immediately declared that the dog would be going home and that I would pray and lay hands on him. My husband paid the visit fee, and we departed.

For two days, I placed my hands on Saadiq's body. In tears I called on the name of Jesus. I remember telling Him, "You have all power. You made the dog, and You know all about him. Please heal him." That evening Saadiq got up, ate, and walked through the house and stood at the front door to go out.

The success of my past continues to strengthen my faith and expectations, for now and the future.

Currently I lay hands on the sick. As I nurse the elderly with the tender touches of my fingers, I call on the name of Jehovah-Rapha. He heals the sick and raises them up.

On occasion I have laid hands on my entire phone book for blessings for each person. Countless times my checkbook, bills, and raffles tickets have been touched in the name of Jesus. In Jesus Christ, I always triumph.

Sometimes I lift my hands and pronounce a wave blessing up and down the Streets of Oakland, California; the schools, my neighbors, addicts, drug dealers, prostitutes, pimps, the homeless, the mentally ill, the incarcerated, and most emphatically, our youth.

In conclusion, while visiting juvenile hall, I recall putting my hand upon the glass windows of the wooden doors, giving benediction to all the faces locked within.

In times like these, it is paramount to bless everyone. I love to lay a firm hand on the heads of our youth, particularly the boys or young men. I beseech Jesus sometimes in silence, but usually out loud so that they might hear and receive the blessing of the Holy Spirit.

Stay-the-Sun Moments

Lord, please don't let my check bounce.
Lord, please give me a little more time before the deadline.
Lord, please don't let the door close before I make it in.
Lord, please let me get through all this traffic on time.

"Then spake Joshua to the Lord in the day when the Lord delivered up the Amorites before the children of Israel, and he said in the sight of Israel, Sun, stand thou still upon Gibeon; and thou, Moon, in the valley of Ajalon. And the sun stood still and the moon stayed, until the people had avenged themselves upon their enemies" (Joshua 10:12–13).

Come, Holy Spirit

Today is June 18, 2007. My feelings, reasoning, and judgment are paralyzed. I just feel the need to personally call upon the Holy Spirit. I could have addressed the third person in the Godhead as the Holy Ghost, or the Comforter. But today, I said out loud, "Come, Holy Spirit, come." These were the words that I spoke at the end of my kitchen table.

Next I proceeded to the bathroom and stood in front of the mirror. I heard the tender voice of the Holy Spirit say, "Ask anything in My name and I will do it." I felt so favored. My mind began to say, "I can do all things through Christ who strengthens me" (Philippians 4:13). I repeated this scripture out loud with confidence.

As I prepared to dress, whatever I looked for, the Holy Spirit directed me. He was my personal butler, my genie. The Comforter's presence brought comfort and peace to my soul.

I strongly believe in the opportunity and the power of an invitation. The invitation can open welcome doors of blessing. Good things are possible.

The gift of the Holy Spirit, which Jesus promised before ascending on high, dwells in the hearts of believers who have accepted Jesus Christ as Savior. Therefore, when you call upon the Holy Spirit, He reigns.

Today I asked the Holy Spirit to give me extra strength and comfort. Today starts the murder trial of my son Aaron. Thank You, Holy Spirit.

PS: Now He is a constant friend.

Who Will Roll the Stone Away?

I know that we all have had thoughts of who will roll the stone away. The vicissitudes of life makes one ponder and even worry about the mountains of life.

Certainly this journey has presented me with mountains, boulders, and stepping stones. Circumstances have taken me to my knees.

The simple blessings of life make me very thankful and grateful, like driving up and a parking space opens just for me. I must admit, I expect to be blessed. Or the time that I needed to pay for parking and had no cash, no checkbook. My roll of quarters saved me. How about thinking to call someone, and before you look up the number, they call you first?

Life delivers some heavy challenges as well. Raising my two young children as a widow was emotionally and financially difficult. A few times I wondered and worried how I would provide food. But I had a little talk with Jesus. Food, baskets, grocery certificates, and invitations to eat out showed up.

During the bereavement of my son, an angel appeared and was faithful. She brought cash: fifty dollars up to two hundred dollars at a time. Sometimes she would come weekly, certainly every two weeks. Her constant generosity overwhelmed me. I was almost ashamed to receive her gifts. She would not let me refuse.

A major mountain in my current life has been my mother's health and care. For the past year, mother's health and quality of life have declined. I, along with siblings and Mom's dedicated RN case manager, escorted and assisted her with numerous doctors' appointments. On mother's last visit to the hospital, she was retained because of congestive heart failure, failing lungs and kidneys, and diabetes.

The family and the medical personnel were at a quandary regarding procedures and where she should be cared for. Mother just wanted to go home. But neither home nor its occupants were equipped for her best care. At times I felt I was not the best daughter because I could not grant my mother's wishes. On Friday, December 7, 2007, I met with the care team. The palliative-care doctor asked my mother, "What do you want?" I wanted to scream. Immediately I left the room and beckoned for the doctor to come. "She wants to go home!" I blurted out. "Let's make it happen," he replied.

Such a weight lifted from my heart; I felt free. We entered the hospital room. I told my mother, "You are going home for Christmas." She had a smile a mile wide. Mother got strong and alert enough to tell everyone, "I'm going home for Christmas!"

As I left the hospital, I asked myself, *What have you done? What will the siblings think? How will I get Mother home?* I didn't have answers, but I was determined to get Mother home for Christmas. I knew that God would work it out.

The family assimilated the decision that Mother would be coming home. They, too, were hopeful. Now Mother's joy was complete. She received an early Christmas gift. Mother went home to be with the Lord on December 10, 2007.

Yes, mountains will appear on this road of life. At times our way appears blocked and hindered. Thanks be to our heavenly Father, that He knows what we need before we ask. The way is already made.

Our positive thinking, prayer, belief, faith, and expectations will enable us to speak to mountains, and they will be removed! We will be able to walk on cobblestones leading to our path of victory.

"And they said among themselves, Who shall roll us away the stone from the door of the sepulchre? And when they looked, they saw that the stone was rolled away: for it was very great" (Mark 16:3–4).

Letter to the President of the United States (Barack Obama)

May 6, 2009

Dear Mr. President:

Congratulations on becoming the forty-fourth president of the United States of America! It is an honor to receive you as the first African American president. Your manifested dream bespeaks this original poem, which I wrote prior to your election. I included it, hoping that you will continue to be inspired as you lead our great nation.

America and the whole world was amazed and proud of your accomplishments on Tuesday, January 20, 2009. I know that the ancestors were shouting and weeping with joy. What a great day!

My family and I watched from the early morning to past midnight, from channel to channel. We as African Americans were elated as we witnessed and identified with your victory.

You walked into history with such grace and dignity. Your lovely wife was right at your side. Your adorable daughters beamed with pride and admiration. Yes, soul has come to the White House!

I close now with a blessing:

May God protect you. May He bestow wisdom and direction for your decisions. My prayer is that He will give you an obedient and loyal staff. I am praying for you and your family always.

"Trust in the Lord with all thine heart, and lean not on your own understanding. In all thy ways acknowledge Him, and He shall direct thy paths" (Proverbs 3:5–6).

And now, "Dare to Dream."

Sincerely,

_____

Tanya R. Crawford

Dare to Dream

Awake from the state of night visions,
Images in a distant fog.

Go ahead, be conscious to call forth
The things that are not.

Your dream comes with great opposition,
Yet with the greatest reward.

Dare to dream.
It is possible!
You have the permission of the almighty Creator.
Bring forth goodness . . .
A dream is born to give.
There is a purpose for your dream:
A desire, a passion,
A burning to be
Fulfilled from the inside out.

Dare to dream.
Disappointment will come:
Lack of motivation, delay,
Distraction, doubt, weakness,
And expect fear to immobilize
The very essence of your dream.
But . . . don't be afraid . . .
take courage.

Dare to dream.
Dream through time, space,
The unseen, the unknown, broken dreams,
Failure, sickness, desertion,
Fallen people, poverty, color,
Gender, status, religion, politics,
Ignorance, hatred, and war.
Yes, even dream through death.

Dare to dream.
Come forth!
Set in order the vision, the dream.
Think it, visualize it, write it, draw it,
Paint it, and speak it.

Visions of My Dreams

Do whatever it takes to plan your dream.
Step by step work your plan.
At scheduled times, at all times,
Anytime is enough time to pursue your dream.

You must stay focused . . .
Ask for help.
Seek guidance.
Receive answers.
Believe always to achieve.
Keep toiling.
Persevere.
Finish.

Evaluate your dream,
Correct your dream,
Bestow your dream.
Oh, the joy of relief,
And the peace of a completed
And well-accomplished dream.

Dare to dream.
Victory!
The reality of your manifested dream,
Your love, creative power,
Invention, the cure, the answer,
The enlightenment, the encouragement,
The hope, the legacy.
The blessing and the gift to humanity
Has been born and delivered through you.

Dare to dream.

Tanya R. Crawford

THE WHITE HOUSE
WASHINGTON

June 25, 2009

Dear Friend:

I want to thank you for your message and for holding me in your prayers. My family and I are honored that so many Americans have supported us in this special way.

Our country faces enormous challenges, but each day I am uplifted by the enduring spirit of the American people. I know that we will meet these challenges if our optimism and hope are met with the necessary will and hard work.

We understand that, *"the strength to go on produces character. Character produces hope. And hope will never let us down"* [Romans 5: 4-5]. In these times of trial and opportunity, I deeply appreciate your prayers for this country, my family, and myself. May God bless you.

Sincerely,

Letter from the President of the United States (Barack Obama)

NOTES

1. 1a, 1b

    "Second Great Migration (African American) Wikipedia, the free encyclopedia"

    http://en.wikipedia.org/wiki/Second_Great_Migration_(African_American)

2. 2a, 2b, 2c, 2d, 2e, 2g, 2f, 2h

    "Picture This: California Perspectives on American History. World War II Homefront Era 1940's: Latin & Black Entertainers Advance on/off stage" 2

    http://www.oaklandmuseumofcalifornia.net/picturethis/pictures/entertainer-paul-robeson-sings-laborers-working-racially-integrated-moore-shipyard-Oakland

    3. "In Loving Memory of Pauline Jordan" (obituary) December 27th, 1900 – June 10th 1989" 3

CPSIA information can be obtained at www.ICGtesting.com
Printed in the USA
LVOW06s0832280913

354496LV00004B/255/P